QUADERNI DI ARABIA ANTICA 2

Alessandra Avanzini

Ancient South Arabian within Semitic and Sabaic within Ancient South Arabian

L'«ERMA» di BRETSCHNEIDER

Quaderni di Arabia Antica 2
series directed by Alessandra Avanzini

Alessandra Avanzini
Ancient South Arabian within Semitic
and Sabaic within Ancient South Arabian

Editing and page layout: Alessandra Lombardi
English text reviser: Geoffrey Phillips

Cover: detail of the inscription RES 4337
(courtesy of Christian J. Robin)

Study published with the contribution of the *European Research Council under the European Union's Seventh Framework Programme (FP7/2007-2013) / Erc grant agreement n° 269774*

ISBN: 978-88-913-0761-3 (paperback)
ISBN: 978-88-913-0762-0 (digital edition)

Contents

1. Introduction

In some of his articles in the last few years, P. Stein (Stein 2012, 2012 a) reiterated his reconstruction of the relationships between Sabaic (SAB) and the North-West Semitic, and between SAB and non-SAB languages in southern Arabia.
In his articles, P. Stein always mentions that there is a different working hypothesis set up by what he calls the 'Pisa school'. It seems though that the arguments put forward by the 'Pisa school' do not seem convincing and did not affect Stein's reconstruction. Once again, it may be worth discussing some aspects of the problem.
Stein's reconstruction is based on a hypothesis initially presented by N. Nebes in 2001.
The linguistic reconstruction proposed by N. Nebes and P. Stein finds justification in the hypothesis put forward by R. Hetzron about the classification of Semitic languages, also confirmed by R. Voigt in 1987 and by N. Nebes in 1994 for what concerns Ancient South Arabian (ASA) languages.
If we accept this general classification framework it seems acceptable to believe that some isoglosses are more relevant than others. According to R. Hetzron (Hetzron 1974) the identification of an innovative area (the Central Semitic) is related to two main isoglosses: the creation of the verbal form yVqtVl and, therefore, the absence in Central Semitic of the verbal opposition *iprus*/*iparras* typical of the Akkadian language, which is reflected in the *yənäggər*/*yəngär* opposition in the Ethiopian language and in Modern South Arabian (MSA); and the presence of the causative prefix and of the third person suffixed pronoun in *h* in the innovative Central Semitic, opposed to the verbal causative and the third person suffixed pronoun in *-s* in the conservative Marginal Semitic.
Incidentally, it is necessary to reiterate from the very beginning that for some scholars the isogloss *iprus*/*iparras vs. yənäggər/yəngär* is questionable – in Ethiopic the form yVqaTTVl could be a secondary creation – and that the *s*>*h* sound change is common throughout Central Semitic.
Moreover, the absence of a yqVttVl form is not definitive in SAB nor in non-SAB languages in Southern Arabia.
Both R. Hetzron and R. Voigt developed their hypotheses when much of the most ancient documentation from ASA kingdoms was still unknown, and when the grammatical structure of non-SAB languages was less known than it is today.
I am trying to argue once again that the hypothesis of a migration of a population of SAB/proto-SAB speakers from the north as an engine for the formation of the ASA culture, is antihistorical and – frankly – quite improbable.
But, the recent 'arrival' of proto-SAB/SAB speakers is not a secondary element in the ASA classification, inside Semitic, offered by N. Nebes and P. Stein. The hypothesis of SAB as a

language belonging to the innovative Central Semitic, opposed to 'archaic' non-SAB languages, loses much of its argumentative strength if we consider the formation of the ASA family as the result of a process developed within southern Arabia, a process that led to the constitution of four written languages including SAB.
Linguistic contacts must also be hypothesized, but a cultural and linguistic contact from South to North cannot be excluded *a priori* from the exclusive advantage of a North to South direction.

The synchronic relationship among ASA languages is an interesting topic both on a linguistic and historical level.
In the formative period of the ASA civilisation, a 'Sabaeization' process in several areas of Yemen, a linguistic and cultural contact, has often been referred in the studies carried out by N. Nebes and P. Stein.
A linguistic and cultural contact between Saba' and non-Sabaean kingdoms is witnessed in the epigraphic documentation, but the time in which the contact occurred, and the content of such contact, still remains to be clarified.
The 'Sabaeization' of non-SAB languages does not depend on a Sabaean political control, nor on a generic cultural prestige imposed on peripheral areas from the newcomers who were technologically and culturally more evolved.
In my opinion, the teaching of writing from a cultural centre of dissemination – which the documentation we have today at our disposal seems to locate in the Jawf region (marked by a strong Sabaean presence) – is the main reason behind the 'Sabaeization' of non-SAB languages.

2. Ancient South Arabian within Semitic

2.1. Nebes and archaeology

N. Nebes hypothesized, supported by archaeological and linguistic proof, that Proto-Canaanite/pre-SAB speakers arrived from the North into a linguistically archaic area. The ancient inhabitants accepted numerous linguistic and cultural elements from the newcomers and vice-versa. Fifteen years ago, when Nebes's article was published, the hypothesis seemed to be supported by the archaeology.

In those years the first archaeological results on the Bronze period in Yemen were published. Neither the results of the excavations of the German team in Sabir, in the South-West area of Yemen (Vogt, Sedov 1998; Vogt, Sedov, Buffa, 2002) nor of the surveys of A. de Maigret (de Maigret 1990) on the plateau, in the area of Dhamār, seemed to imply any evident relation with ASA culture. The formation of ASA culture outside Arabia was an idea strongly supported by almost all archaeologists working in Yemen at the end of the last century, who believed that a migration from the north of groups of peoples, in the second millennium, brought to Yemen building techniques, different types of pottery, and script.

According to N. Nebes the analysis of the linguistic situation within Yemen supported the migratory model as proposed by the archaeologists.

Today the caution of N. Nebes when expounding his hypothesis of migration and cultural transfer from Saba' to the ancient inhabitants of the Yemen is highly appreciated.

N. Nebes emphasizes in his article that his reconstruction is a working hypothesis, in need of clear historical evidence but especially of data from north Arabia.

Moreover, 15 years ago when N. Nebes wrote his contribution, a long chronological interval seemed to exist between the Aramaic and Canaanite epigraphic documentation and the ASA one. Some epigraphic ASA texts from the first half of the eighth century are still not known, nor had a date at the end of the second millennium been demonstrated for the most ancient texts in minuscule script.

Also for the learning of script in South Arabia, once again I believe it is worth emphasizing Nebes's cautious approach. He found it unlikely that script technique was brought directly by the proto-Canaanite/pre-SAB populations migrating from the North to Yemen, but it had to be set in a previous time:

> *Die Übernahme des Alphabets in Südarabien muss mitnichten Hand in Hand mit der Einwanderung einer protokanaanäischen-vorsabäischen Population gegangen sein. Viel wahrscheinlicher ist es, dass die Schrift in irgendeiner Form nach Süden gewandert ist, vermutlich über die Weihrauchstrasse, die sicherlich bereits vor der Spätbronzezeit Südarabien mit den nordwestsemitischen Raum verbunden hat.* (Nebes 2001, 430)

To make sure that his hypothesis of a migration from the north and the integration of the newcomers was credible, N. Nebes felt the need for a time interval: in my opinion a very necessary need that was later forgotten by P. Stein.

For a long time, the archaeological results have created a serious problem for an endogenous reconstruction hypothesis.
The lack of a past, with a clear relation with the following ASA culture, was an element that worked against a linguistic and cultural continuity inside Yemen.
The idea of a civilization born from nowhere and within a short time span seemed to be supported by the lack of evident relations with the proto-historic period.
Today, thanks to the results of archaeological research on the plateau of the mission of Chicago (Wilkinson 2005) and the overall picture of the endogenous formation process of settlements on the plateau and on the edge of the desert provided by J. Schiettecatte (Mouton, Schiettecatte 2014) we have the chance to see, from an archaeological viewpoint, a general reconstruction opposed to the one presented only few years ago.
J. Schiettecatte (in Mouton, Schiettecatte 2014, 170):

> Continuity of settlement between the end of the Bronze Age and the early Iron Age can be seen in the occupation of the land and in various elements of the material cultural. This leads us to reject the migration hypothesis that turns South Arabia into a dead-end receiving populations coming from the southern Levant in the early 1st millennium BC.

The excavations carried out in the last few years show how the capital cities of the ASA kingdoms demonstrated a continuity with settlements from the second millennium.
For example, regarding Barāqish:

> *Un sondage réalisé en 2007 par A. de Maigret a permis d'attester une occupation continue sur le site du XIIIe siècle av. J.-C.* (Schiettecatte 2011, 53)

Before the historical Marib, there is a more ancient city of which the social organisation is unknown, but it certainly already existed and in the same area of the historical Sabaean capital city. Archaeology still has not concluded its discoveries and despite the gravity of the current unstable political situation in Yemen that caused the suspension of excavations, it is now possible to have an overview of the archaeological data leading to a hypothesis of a long internal process before the formation of the ASA culture.

2.2. Nebes's linguistic hypothesis

For N. Nebes the SAB linguistic similarities with Proto-Canaanite seem to be neither sporadic nor random. They are not justifiable by a genetic similarity but only through a geographic proximity between the two languages in their past. From this observation the hypothesis of a migration from the north of Proto-Canaanite/pre-SAB speakers towards southern Arabia is derived.
Regarding the general classification of SEM languages, the close resemblance between SAB and Canaanite was functional to the reconstruction of an innovative Central Semitic as put forward by R. Hetzron.

N. Nebes already supported such hypothesis in a 1994 article with the reconstruction of the imperfect with a /qtVl/ base in ASA.
This isogloss is fundamental for R. Hetzron, who saw in the innovative creation of the form yVqtVl one of the main elements, perhaps the main element, to define the Central Semitic opposed to an archaic, Marginal Semitic.
The importance attached to this isogloss by the supporters of a Central Semitic opposed to a Marginal and archaic Semitic, is reaffirmed in some recent studies.

For example, J. Huehnergard (Huehnergard 2005, 160-161) states:

> By examining forms of weak verbs, Nebes demonstrated that none of the languages for which there is sufficient evidence – Sabaean, Minaean, and Qatabanian – exhibits the form *yVqattVl*; the imperfective form of the verb is, instead, *yaqtulu*. This is very significant; it means that these languages participated in the principle innovation that characterizes the Central Semitic branch.

Also R. Hasselbach (Hasselbach 2012, 164) emphasizes that:

> The genetic classification of OSA depends on whether its verbal system corresponds to that of Central Semitic, or that of Modern South Arabian and Ethiopian Semitic.

But, the isogloss between Ethiopic/MSA *vs.* Akkadian is not so indisputable.
I would like to quote here D. Cohen 1984, who starting from the question:

> *Les formes à gémination de la deuxième radicale de l'éthiopien et de l'akkadien procèdent-elles d'un même prototype ?* (Cohen 1984, 63)

arrives at a completely different conclusion.
In fact, considering that:

> *L'éthiopien avait effacé en quelque sorte le rapport sémantique qui caractérisait les thèmes anciennement intensifs (CaCCaC et CēCaC) comme thèmes fondés par rapport à un thème de fondement CaCaC* ... (Cohen 1984, 67)

then:

> *Le renouvellement de l'inaccompli a pu s'opérer facilement par l'introduction du thème intensif* yəqattəl (< *yuqattilu) *dans la conjugaison simple* [... ...]. yəqattəl, *à la fois inaccompli indicatif de la forme base et jussif de la conjugaison anciennement intensive, ne peut s'expliquer phonétiquement que par une forme antérieure* *yuqittil(u). *Cette forme* yuqattil(u) *est précisément la forme de l'inaccompli de la conjugaison intensive du sémitique. Elle ne peut pas correspondre à la forme du présent akkadien* iparras *qui n'aurait pu être en éthiopien que* *yaparras *ou* *yəparras. (Cohen 1984, 67)

The strength of the absence in ASA of yVqattVl form is such that N. Nebes can state that undoubtedly the Ethiopian language and MSA do not derive from SAB, though these languages could derive from the archaic linguistic substratum of Yemen.

N. Nebes found archaeological evidence for his hypothesis of the Ethiopic language deriving from the pre-SAB archaic substratum in the archaeological contacts between Sabir culture and Africa (Buffa, Vogt 2001).
In particular, for what concerns MSA, I believe it is wrong to affirm in an apodictic way that since in ASA the yVqattVl form has not been proven (thus transforming Nebes's reconstructive hypothesis into an irrefutable evidence) ASA cannot be the ancestor of MSA.
Sometimes all is needed is a pinch of common sense.
The genetic relation between ASA and MSA is certainly complex and the comparison between oral texts from semi-nomadic populations, recorded in recent times, with public, formal texts (Macdonald 2015, 3-7) from more than 2000 years ago is not easy and calls for a precise methodological care.
But to exclude *a priori* any possible genetic relation seems to me highly improbable.

N. Nebes is very cautious in defining the archaic linguistic substratum in Yemen.
The migration of the Sabaeans from the north did not move towards an 'empty' country, but to a place already inhabited by speakers of an archaic Semitic language.
While for P. Stein the non-SAB languages are 'archaic', vis-a-vis the 'innovative' SAB, in my opinion, it seems clear that N. Nebes considers that the archaic linguistic substratum in Southern Arabia is to be identified with something else and not with the non-SAB ASA languages, the Minaic (MIN), the Qatabanic (QAT), the Ḥaḍramitic (HAD).
As mentioned, on the basis of the archaeological discoveries in those years, N. Nebes hypothesized that the culture of the late Bronze in Sabir had to be linked to populations speaking an archaic Semitic language established in Yemen, before the arrival of Sabaeans.
The *-k* ending of the first and second person for the suffixed form of the verbs and the broken plurals are a linguistic proof of the existence of such archaic Semitic pre-SAB.
Incidentally, it is not quite right to consider the suffix *-k* and the broken plural as 'archaic' linguistic traits of Semitic. In Akkadian there is *-k* (first person) *vs.* *-t* (second person); in North-West Semitic and in Arabic we have a paradigmatic levelling in *-t*, and in South Semitic in *-k*. The broken plurals can be either shared retentions or areal developments. But, in any case, the SAB, from the most ancient documentation and unlike the North-West Semitic, is involved in the development of the broken plurals.
This is not the place to discuss the Afro-Asiatic origin of the broken plural, or the distinctive importance of a plural form based on its own logical categories differing from the external plural (Corriente 2013, with previous references) even if the broken plural is an isogloss able to define a Southern Semitic area within the Semitic languages.
Surely, the hypothesis would be far more convincing if the two 'archaic' traits that N. Nebes mentions (*-k* and the broken plural) were not present in SAB, the newly arrived language from the north; for him, the archaic features (*-k* and the broken plurals) are present in SAB thanks to a contact with the speakers archaic Semitic languages in Yemen.
The linguistic contact may have clearly advanced together with the cultural integration of the newcomers as bearers of a more advanced culture but, in the case of languages in contact, loans from one language to the other do not move from one to the other haphazardly, but they are usually imposed upon by the stronger culture onto the weaker one.
The presence of the suffix *-k* and of broken plural, from the most ancient SAB documentation – *-k* in the sticks written in Early Sabaic, the broken plural in inscriptions from the beginning of

the 8th century – are linguistic elements that cannot be underestimated and that linked the SAB to the other ASA languages more than with the North-West Semitic.

Moreover, the absence of yVqattVl in ASA is hypothetical.
To demonstrate that there is no indication for a pattern analogous to Ethiopic *yəqattəl* in any ASA language N. Nebes (Nebes 1994) analysed verbs of *mediae infirmae* to see if the ASA verbal system was similar to the Ethiopian and to the MSA, languages that present the *nagara* past verbal form, the present indicative *yənäggər* and the subjunctive *yəngär*.
N. Nebes compares examples of subjunctive/jussive with examples of the indicative for the verbs of *mediae infirmae* and comes to the conclusion that both in the indicative and subjunctive, the weak consonant may not appear in writing.
SAB verbal system is, then, comparable to the verbal system of Central Semitic and not to the Marginal Semitic verbal system.
But, if we accept A.F.L. Beeston's statement (Beeston 1984, 16) – also supported by P. Stein (Stein 2003, 192, n. 218) – "the difference in writing of the imperfect with a second weak letter is purely graphical and not morphological", the whole reconstruction by N. Nebes loses much of its strength.
Moreover, P. Stein in more recent times (Stein 2011, 1061) cited an example of a verb of *mediae infirmae* which presents a defective writing in the jussive form: *l-ys²mn wfy* ..."may He set up the well-being of ..." (Ja 611, 16-17) and a full writing in the indicative: *ḏt s²ym w-ys²ymn wfy* ... "that He has set up and will set up the well-being of ..." (München VM 91-315 336).
I would not infer from this example that we have found, in the end, a clear proof of the presence of the opposition *yənäggər/yəngär* in SAB and that, as a consequence, the classification of ASA languages inside the Central Semitic and the absence of a genetic relation between ASA and MSA are wrong hypotheses.
It is true that the example is particularly important because it compares two different typologies of texts: a public text and a text in minuscule script, free from strict writing rules. A morphologic opposition between subjunctive/jussive and indicative seems marked in SAB and the indicative *ys²ymn* may recall the form yVqattVl.
I would rather not fall into the trap of an easy general reconstruction based on a single example. The uncertainty already mentioned in ascertaining if the opposition of full writing and defective writing actually underlies a morphologic phenomenon must not be forgotten.
I cannot state that we have found a proof of the presence in SAB of some archaic linguistic traits, including the diagnostic verbal isogloss that characterizes the Marginal Semitic.
For the time being it is necessary to shed light on data without putting forward easy conclusions; it would be better to show less self-assurance.
ASA script does not allow us to find definitive proof of the grammatical phenomenon; and the 'rule' might be proven wrong in the future, on the basis of further examples over the one previously cited.

2.3. Stein's hypothesis on a relationship between Sabaic and Aramaic

The strenuous work, two fundamental books (Stein 2003, Stein 2010) has made Peter Stein a leading scholar for SAB grammar, but, his articles of historical linguistics often seem less fortunate (obviously, in my opinion).

P. Stein recalls the linguistic evidence about the strong link between SAB and North-West Semitic brought about by N. Nebes (Stein 2012 a, 46, n. 48). It appears though that P. Stein is dangerously led towards substituting Nebes's proto-Canaanite with Aramaic, *tout court*. In his articles, Stein uses 'proto-' only before MIN, he no longer uses proto-Sabaic or proto-Canaanite, but only Sabaic and Aramaic.

Furthermore, it is evident that for P. Stein the archaic substratum in Yemen is to be identified with the non-SAB languages. The opposition is between SAB (innovative) *vs.* non-SAB (archaic). Even in this case one must regret the caution of N. Nebes in defining the archaic linguistic substratum in Yemen.

The parallels between Aramaic and Sabaic are made clear in the most recent article by P. Stein, co-authored with Ingo Kottsieper (Kottsieper, Stein 2014).

I. Kottsieper and P. Stein (KS) insist on the credibility of an important migration of populations in order to justify the linguistic situation of ASA:

> The seeming paradox of a continuity of South Arabian civilization during the second millennium along with a clearly Central (or North-west) Semitic setting of some parts of this culture could well be solved by assuming migration, not of entire civilizations but of a small group, the Sabaeans. (KS, 85)

Resorting to an arrival from the outside to explain a process in the ancient world is certainly an obsolete model, and the majority of historians do not accept it anymore. However, it does have the advantage of being an 'easy' model.

SAB is different from other ASA languages because it presents the 'recent' prefix of the causative verb and of the suffixed pronoun in *-h*, opposed to non-SAB languages with the prefix and the suffix in sibilant, so it is an innovative central linguistic area, surrounded by archaic marginal linguistic areas. Therefore, SAB speakers did settle in Yemen in a more recent period.

As has already happened before, sometimes historical linguistics forgets about history.

The date when SAB migration took place – note, right in the middle of Near East historical period – is a nullifying element.

KS cannot place the Sabaean arrival too early in time because of its supposed direct comparison with Aramaic.

To ensure that the hypothesis is coherent, the migration must be set at the end of the 2nd millennium. Unlike N. Nebes, P. Stein has at his disposal the epigraphic documentation and the texts in minuscule writing from the beginning of the first millennium (Drewes *et alii* 2013), contemporary – if not older – to the Old Aramaic epigraphic documentation.

For the linguistic contact to be credible within Yemen (i.e. 'archaic' traits from non-SAB languages to SAB), time is a crucial element which is persistently ignored by P. Stein.

The comparison led by KS between the Sabaeans who "introduced the use of script in their new homeland and thus laid the basis for a common writing culture of peoples speaking completely different languages" (KS, 85) with "the common acceptance of Latin languages and script in Medieval Europe, or the advance of English in the former colonies of the British Empire" (KS, 85, n. 21) is wrong and devoid of any historical basis.

Certainly, English does not borrow morphological traits from the many languages spoken in India!

The need to look for a time interval so that a complex process could take place, led J. Pirenne to offer her hypothesis of a short chronology. She was firmly convinced that Sabaeans arrived from the north, but felt the need to define a long period (500 years) so that ASA alphabetical writing – which she thought stemmed directly from Phoenician writing – could thrive in southern Arabia.
To accept a long chronology, as P. Stein obviously does, does not simply mean to change the dates, but to revise the credibility of the proposed process.
The (almost) contemporaneity of the processes in the formation of states and the recording of the epigraphic sources in the Yemen and in the Syrian-Palestinian area, makes the hypothesis of a migration from the north absolutely unrealistic.
If this was true, something more consistent on a cultural level than the *h-* morpheme clearly would have emerged from SAB sources!
Sabaeans are an integral part and the engine of the creation of the ASA culture.

The migration model proposed by N. Nebes and P. Stein is conditioned by an implicit usage of the genealogical model which frequently, on a historical level, implies the migratory model (Mazzini 2005, 225), as is clear from the question posed by KS: "how and when these Central Semitic languages found their way to South Arabia?" (KS, 83-84).
South Arabia is not the cradle of Semitic languages, so the first Semitic language speakers 'arrived' very slowly in South Arabia during a very long period. After 3000 BC when desertification in the Arabian peninsula intensified reaching its present levels, the linguistic story within Yemen is primarily an internal matter. From this period contacts between South and North and vice-versa produced "a developing linguistic area, a *continuum*, albeit at a different rhythm and under different cultural conditions, in direct connection with the proto-Semitic matrix, but under unequal pressure from linguistic contact and wave transfer" (Del Olmo Lete 2013, 116).

Let us return to KS's article.
The parallel between Aramaic and Sabaic is argued by KS both on historical and linguistic level.
For KS the Aramaean kingdoms like the Sabaean one were formed thanks to a migration of people:

> Both the Aramaeans and their language are new elements of the Syrian-Mesopotamian society, which arrived there only at the end of the second millennium and probably originated from an area south of Mesopotamia somewhere at the eastern fringes of Syria-Palestine or even further south. (KS, 82)

That is perhaps an old model to explain the formation of Aramean states. It is sufficient to recall here an opposite opinion:

> It may be closer to the reality to consider that there were no great shifts of population after the collapse of the Late Bronze Age society. [...] The Aramaization of Syria results less from the conquest of the region by Aramaean invaders than from the emergence of a new elite whose legitimacy had its roots in the tribal system and who identified themselves as Aramaeans. (Bunnens 2000, 16)

For KS, as the SAB is different from the other ASA languages, so the Aramaic is different from the other North-West Semitic languages.
Since the last decades of the last century, for the Aramaic language a more 'processual' view of language development has been gaining ground (Garr 1985), whereby the distinctive features of Old Aramaic may be seen as emerging initially from a North-West Semitic linguistic continuum (Fales 2011, 578).

I would like here briefly to examine the list of isoglosses presented to support their hypothesis in KS.
At the very beginning, two observations seem necessary.
As mentioned before, if the intrusive arrival of a population is to be linguistically credible, the 'innovative' linguistic traits, shared with the north, should be a typical trait of the newcomers, and not common to all ASA. The risk is to confuse isoglosses that are common to the whole ASA linguistic family, which define its place inside Semitic, with isoglosses that characterize SAB only.
Moreover, if the purpose of KS was to demonstrate the strong links between SAB and Aramaic, it is frankly bizarre to find among the isoglosses which separate Aramaic from the other North-West Semitic languages the lexical isoglosses Aramaic/MSA *br* 'son' and *tryn* 'two' (KS, 83, n. 5).
If KS wish to demonstrate the genetic connection of Sabaic and Aramaic, they can use only innovative isoglosses shared by the two languages, neither those which are present in the other ASA languages nor in the Marginal Semitic.

1. A well-known feature which separates all other South Arabian languages from Sabaic is the formation of the causative stem and the third person pronouns with a sibilant, not with /h/

That is an isogloss useful inside ASA, but as already I said, the *s>h* sound change is common throughout Central Semitic and, in any case, cannot suggest a closer relationship with Aramaic. Why Aramaic and not Dadanitic? Or Hebrew? Or why not a conservative trait in Sabaic connected with the causative/pronoun in *h* in Amorite ?

2. The postponed article

The postponed article is shared by all south Arabian languages, and so cannot serve to connect Aramaic with Sabaic. Moreover, the article is mostly absent in the earliest Aramaic inscriptions, implying that it developed after the diversification of Aramaic.

3. The number of consonants

Aramaic and Sabaic exhibited twenty-nine consonantal phonemes.
The number of consonants is absolutely irrelevant, especially considering that both languages seem to preserve reflexes of all the Proto-Semitic consonants. No shared innovations have taken place and therefore there is no reason to assume a connection between SAB and Aramaic.
Incidentally, some notes about what KS are saying on the HAD phonological system seem necessary:

> While the immediately neighbouring languages, Minaic and Qatabanic, like Sabaic have preserved the full consonantal inventory, the most remote language, Hadramitic, shows remarkable deficiencies: not only does it lack the fricative interdentals /ḏ/ and /ṯ/ (being merged with the corresponding sibilants /z/ and /ś/, respectively), but it also confuses the emphatics /ṣ/ and /ẓ/, thus strongly recalling the consonantal system of Ethiopic. (KS, 85)

The merging of *ḏ* in *z* and *ẓ* in *ṣ* is a banal evolution attested also in the linguistic history of SAB (Stein 2003, 24-25 and 28-29).
As is well known, *ṯ* vs s^3 and s^3 vs *ṯ* in HAD have to do primarily with different writing schools, not only with a close realization of the two phonemes (Prioletta 2006).

4. Verbal system

For the verb in P. Stein (Stein 2012 a) quoted two syntactic features, already brought by N. Nebes in 2001, as examples of comparison between the North-West Semitic and Sabaic: the imperfect-consecutive, and the infinitive as finite verb.
For the imperfect-consecutive there is a parallelism with the Hebrew and Old Aramaic (Fales 2011, 568), but this construction is not known in SAB only, but also in the other ASA languages.
The infinitive as finite verb has only one possible comparison with absolute and construct infinitive in Hebrew and in Aramaic, but the absolute/construct infinitive in Hebrew and in Aramaic has no relationship with the syntactic construction *finite verb + infinitives*, common to all ASA languages and without terms of comparison outside ASA.

KS maintain that the morphology of the SAB verbal conjugation is the same as the Aramaic:

> The verbal system is exactly the same in both languages (three base stems G, D, and H and three corresponding reflexives, formed by infixed or prefixed t, as well as passive forms, but not lengthened stems and no N-stems). (KS, 84)

Perhaps that statement is a little hastily written.

KS forgot the form *s^1t-* for causative-reflexive form attested in SAB and in all the Southern Semitic and unknown in Aramaic and in North Western Semitic.
This forgetfulness on the part of P. Stein seems to me really very serious. A great part of his discussion on the opposition SAB/non-SAB is based on the opposition *h/s*. In his reconstruction of the SAB verbal system, *s^1t-* is a form of causative-reflexive; the presence of s^1 cannot be underestimated.
For the N-Stem and L-stem, we can quote some observations from J. Huehnergard, A. Rubin. For the N-Stem:

> We would not therefore group together Akkadian, Hebrew, and Arabic, since the N-Stem is undoubtedly a Proto-Semitic feature that has been lost or marginalized independently in the other languages. Nor would we group together those languages that have lost this form; a shared loss is not usually diagnostic for subgrouping. (Huehnergard, Rubin 2011, 266)

For the L-stem we can start from A.F.L. Beeston's observation:

> In Ṣayhadic, the existence of such forms cannot be detected because of the vowelless orthography of those languages, and indirect evidence is very scant. (Beeston 1984, 12-13)

Then we can quote again J. Huehnergard, A. Rubin:

> These forms probably reflect a Proto-Semitic feature that was lost in Akkadian and, with rare exception, in Proto-Northwest Semitic. Their presence in Arabic is a shared retention from an earlier ancestor, not an innovation shared exclusively by Arabic and Ethiopian Semitic. (Huehnergard, Rubin 2011, 291)

KS wish to see a genetic connection between Aramaic and Sabaic because of several common features, but they downplay all the differences between Aramaic and Sabaic: the plural system of the nouns, the loss of a productive system of case endings in Aramaic, the infinitive (the Aramaic presents an innovative prefix *m-* unknown in SAB), the form *hitp*^{e}ʿl *vs.* *s*^{1}*tf*ʿ*l*, etc.

A special relationship between those two Semitic languages is, in my opinion, completely arbitrary.

ASA languages, SAB included, seem to be formed in southern Arabia, and we can presume the existence of a proto-ASA, indeed already divided in different dialects.
Having said this, the relationship between SAB and the Near Eastern world beyond Arabia is more complex than I once thought.
For a historical reconstruction, probably my hypothesis of the existence of an already well-consolidated Sabaean state in the south, (thanks to the development of agriculture, which then came into contact with the north between the end of the second and the beginning of the first millennium), represents an equally great simplification like the one, already mentioned, which hypothesizes a recent arrival from the north of Sabaean populations.
It can be presumed that, during the formative phase of ASA culture, movements of peoples from south to north and vice versa took place. These were displacements involving temporary settlements, close interactions, and the probable presence of ASA-speaking enclaves for a period in the north.
The Sabaeans were the principle actors during this phase of cultural intermingling.
The recent archaeological discoveries in Tayma' and in other oases from north Arabia provide evidence of a cultural linking element between northern and southern areas of the peninsula.
That there were contacts between Tayma', Palestine and Mesopotamia is convincingly demonstrated by cultural elements, beginning with the history of writing. I do not know whether the hypothesis recently put forward by Ch. Robin (Robin 2008) – according to which Tayma' could have been a centre from which South Semitic writing spread – is correct, but it would be consistent with our reconstruction of an extended zone of cultural contacts between the southern and the northern regions of the peninsula.
The hope could be shared, as expressed by N. Nebes, that a better knowledge of the history of northern Arabia, in the second half of the second millennium, will clarify the mechanisms of contact between cultures.

3. Excursus on the prefixed verbal forms in Early Sabaic and in Qatabanic

Before stating that SAB verbal system is identical to the Aramaic one, J. Tropper's hypothesis (Tropper 1997) should be taken into consideration about two forms of prefixed conjugation of Semitic in the second millennium, which finds in ASA some interesting supporting evidence. As is known, the prefixed conjugation of verb in SAB presents a form with *-n* suffix (*yfʿln*) together with the form *yfʿl*.

According to J. Tropper, the two forms, at least at the beginning, could correspond to two forms of the verbal system attested in the Semitic of the second millennium: the short prefixed form in SAB (without *-n*) seemed to have expressed a perfective aspect and a past tense; the long prefixed form (with *-n* suffix), an imperfective aspect and a non-anterior tense.

Obviously enough, the hypothesis of a diachronic reconstruction of the verbal system proposed by J. Tropper seems to adapt perfectly to the hypothesis of a process inside Yemen, before the formation of the historical documentation, and would be incompatible with the hypothesis of a 'recent' arrival of the Sabaeans.

It is true that the use of a prefixed conjugation – as proposed by J. Tropper – does not seem to have unambiguous supporting evidence in the long history of SAB documentation (see also R. Hasselbach 2012, 183), and that it is not easy to find a functional difference between one form and the other, often used indifferently in similar contexts (Nebes 1994 a, 202).

If the opposition in proto-ASA was true, in Early SAB we would find some examples of *yfʿl* as past.

3.1. Early Sabaic prefixed verbal forms

I'd like to discuss some examples, in order not to arrive at the *definition* of a grammar rule, but to recognize some *tendencies* in the use of *fʿl vs. yfʿl vs. yfʿln* in Early SAB.

1. *yfʿl* as 'past'

We have very few but meaningful examples of this value for *yfʿl*.

As we will see, the prefixed form is connected with what precedes, so normally it is preceded by the conjunction *w-* but this is not the case in the two following examples:

(1) RES 3945, 16: *w-hgrn Ns²n yhḥrm bn mwfṭm* "and the city of Nashshān, he annihilated with fire".

For DAI Ṣirwāḥ 2005-50 a complete edition is not published (Nebes 2007, Nebes 2011), but, thanks to the kindness of N. Nebes, I was able to check the whole text.

In this inscription from the middle of the 8th century, no prefixed forms are attested; a punctual comparison with RES 3945, 16 is meaningful:
DAI Ṣirwāḥ 2005-50, 2: *w-Tmnʿ-m hḥrm bn mṯbrm w-mwfṭm* "and Timnaʿ he annihilated with destruction and fire"; at line 4 the same construction: *w-Kmnhw-m hḥrm bn mṯbrm w-mwfṭm* "and Kamna he annihilated with destruction and fire".

So *yhḥrm* in RES 3945 = *hḥrm* in DAI Ṣirwāḥ 2005-50.

(2) RES 3945, 18: *w-nqm yhqm ḥr S¹bʾ w-Ḍhr ḏ-ʾmnt Krbʾl ḏ-yhrgw* "with a vengeance he avenged free men of Sabaʾ and *Ḍhr*, who are under the protection of Karibil, who had been killed".

In DAI Ṣirwāḥ 2005-50, 1: *w-nqm Ykrbmlk w-S¹bʾ* "he avenged *Ykrbmlk* and Sabaʾ".
This example is not so sure: in *yqhm* the first radical *n* would be assimilated and that is irregular in Early SAB. So, we can translate RES 3945, 18-19: "he avenged *Yhqm*, the free man of Sabaʾ and *Ḍhr*, who is under the protection of Karibil, whom they killed". Incidentally, for the problem we are discussing, *ḏ-yhrgw*, also in this translation, is to be translated with a past.
There are some reasons for preferring the first translation: a proper name, formed with the same root NQM, seems very unlikely and in the other attestations of *ḥr* in RES 3945, the noun seems a collective and not a singular one (ll. 6, 9, 12: *ḥr-hw w-ʿbd-hw* "his freemen and his slaves"). If the translation is right *yqhm* connects the sentence with the preceding sentence: "when he broke *S¹bl* and *Hrm* and *Fnnn* and took possession of all their irrigated lands and burned the cities of *S¹bl* and the cities of *Hrm* and the cities of *Fnnn* and killed three thousand (3,000) of them and killed their kings and took prisoner five thousand (5,000) of them and seized fifteen thousand (15,000) of their livestock and imposed upon them a tribute for Almaqah and Sabaʾ so with a vengeance he avenged free men of Saba and *Ḍhr*, who were under the protection of Karibil, who had been killed".

2. *w-fʿl vs. w-yfʿl*
The use of *w-yfʿl* instead of *w-fʿl* is tied to a stylistic feature, its use specifies a narrative articulation in the story, and not to a different tense of the verb. This is not such an original observation, it was already presented some years ago by Y. Gruntfest (Gruntfest 1999).
In any case *w-yfʿl* strongly related the verb to the previous sentence. A meaning of 'circumstantial past' is sometimes the more convenient translation.

(3) RES 3945, 14: *w-ywm ns²ʾ ṯnym mns²ʾm w-ygnʾ gnʾm* "and when he made a second expedition and (during this expedition) he constructed a wall".
vs.
(4) RES 3945, 17: *w-gnʾ Ns²qm* "And he walled Nashq".
In this case, we are dealing with a new action of the king. The previous sentence speaks of the city of Kamna.
(5) RES 3946, 3-4: *w-s²ʾm Ḫdnn ʾdm Ḫḍrhmw ḏ-Mfʿlm w-Gbrm ʾdm Yʿṯq ḏ-Ḫwln ḏ-Yrrt w-ys³f-mw ḥw-hw Fys²n* "and he bought *Ḫdnn*, the vassals of *Ḫḍrhmw*, he of *Mfʿlm* and *Gbrm*, the vassals of *Yʿʿṯq*, he of *Ḫwln* of *Yrrt*, so he augmented his free men of Fayshān".

vs.

(6) RES 3946, 8 *w-ws*^{3}*f ḥw-hw Fys*^{2}*n ʾdm hs*^{2}*ʾm-hw Ḥḍrhmw ḏ-Mfʿlm* "And he augmented his free men of Fayshān with the vassals whom *Ḥḍrhmw*, he of *Mfʿlm*, had sold to him".

In this case, we have a new sentence not connected with the previous one.

RES, following N. Rhodokanakis, reads: *w-(y)s*^{3}*f ḥw-hw Fys*^{2}*n* ... but the here proposed reading is sure (see fig. 1).

Figure 1 - RES 3946 (courtesy of Khaldon Noman).

Some examples of a strong 'circumstantial past' meaning are attested in RES 3945:

(7) RES 3945, 1 *w-yʾtmmw w-yḥtẓyw mns*^{2}*ʾ-hmw* "so that they might gather (under his leadership) with successful auspices in their expeditions";

(8) RES 3945, 2: *w-yns*^{2} *ʾs*^{1}*m l-mtʿ qny-hw* "so that every man acted to safeguard its (of Sabaʾ) property";

(9) RES 3945, 2: *w-yhṯb mwy ḏbh-hw*, "so that he might assign the waters of his plain";

(10) RES 3945,16: *w-ʿtb bn Ns*^{2}*n ʾl wḍʾt s*^{2}*ft-hmw ns*^{1}*r-n ʾlʾltn w-yhrgw* "he requested from Nashshān those, whose fate had been decided by (under the authority of) the gods, and so were killed".

The action is not just coordinated with what precedes it but it is a circumstance, a consequence of the former action.

3. *ḏ-yfʿl*

In the following example in RES 3945, it seems that the use of *ḏ-yfʿl* instead of *ḏ-fʿl* is functional with a strong iterated/durative value of the verb: the action has a value forever: "he did and forever he will do":

(11) RES 3945, 3-4: *w-bḍʿ b-ʿl-hmw b-ʿm s*^{3}*lʾ-hmw bqrm w-s*^{1}*frtm ḏ-yḫbw b-ʿm s*^{3}*lʾ-hmw* "and imposed them, in addition to their tribute, livestock of large and small size, of which they are (and will be) indebted in addition to their tribute".

4. *yfʿln* with a durative value

(12) RES 3945, 2: *w-ḥmy ḥrt-hw ʿhl l-Mʾwdn bn k-ḏ tḍʾn brḥm l-ḏhbnhn* "he protected his dam ʿhl up to *Mʾwdn* (or: up to the boundary) in such a way that (the water) is not flowing uncontrolled toward the two plains";

(13) RES 3946, 3: *ʾs*^{1}*rr yrdnn* "valleys that are extending".

5. *yfʿln vs. yfʿl* in the Early SAB legal texts

The opposition between the two forms (*yfʿl vs. yfʿln*) is functional not only with an aspectual value, but also with the text syntax, in particular in the legal texts.

In the legal texts there is a sequence of rules associated: *when he is* (*will be*) *doing something* (*yfʿln*) *then he has to do something* (*l-yfʿl*); *if he is* (*will be*) *doing something* (*yfʿln*) *then he has to do something* (*l-yfʿl*). In addition to the various conjunctions, the tense of the verb is functional with the clarification of the syntax of the rule.

(14) CIH 563+956, 5: *ḏ-(y)ʿdwn b-ʿly ḏn mḫrn w-l ys*^{1}*tʿḏb-hw* "whoever is committing an offence against this edict, then let there be demanded a penalty against him";

(15) RES 3947, 9-10: *w-ʾhn yʿkrn Ys*^{2}*hrmlk w-l yndʾ mwm* "and whenever *Ys*^{2}*hrmlk* is raising an objection, then let him make water flow".

(16) MAFRAY-Ḥuṣn Al-Sāliḥ 1, 7-8: *w-k ʾḥd yflqn f-ʾl ybdr ʾḥd ʾḥd* "when one is opening (the floodgate), then let no one anticipate the other".

In the former examples we have *yfʿln* in the protasis and *yfʿl* in the apodosis, with a modal value, in the following example the two verbs are in the indicative and the syntax is clear only thanks to the two verbal forms:

(17) MAFRAY-Ḥuṣn Al-Sāliḥ 1, 8-10: *w-s*^{3}*ʿ mwy yḍʾ bn ... s*^{3}*ʿ-hw yḍʾn bn ...* "the quantity of water which exits from … the same quantity will be exiting from …".

3.2. Qatabanic prefixed verbal forms

I have already discussed the QAT verb (Avanzini 2009): the QAT prefixed verbal forms work quite clearly: *yfʿl/w-yfʿlw*, with a stylistic connotation, as past, *b-yfʿl/b-yfʿlwn* as present in relative sentences, *l- yfʿl/l- yfʿlwn* as jussive.

I had already corrected the impossible form: *l-b-yfʿl* in RES 4337C, 14-15 (Avanzini 2014): *w-ʾl b-ymtʿ* instead of *w-n-l b-ymtʿ*.

Here, I wish to return briefly on the few QAT examples of *yfʿl/yfʿlwn* without *b* or *l*.

In these cases in 2009 I give a definition for these forms as narrative-imperfective. Today, I think that the durative aspect of these verbs is to be emphasized.

1. *yfʿl/yfʿlwn* in relative sentences

Again, we have to be cautious.
In some examples the forms *yfʿl/yfʿlwn* are attested in relative sentences. The choice to use the verbal forms without *b-* is it meaningful or is it a lapse of the scribe?

(18) RES 3878, 3: *w-kl ʾs²ʿbm ymlk Ydʿʾb* "all the tribes on which *Ydʿʾb* is (and will be) reigning";
(19) RES 4931, 2: *ʾs¹dm ys³mk bn* … "anyone who is (and will be) going up from …"

(20) In RES 4337A, 26-28 the lecture of the editors, accepted in CSAI, was:

26 *l-yḫrṯ ḫms¹y wrqm*
27 *l-mlk Qtbn w-ʿhr S²mr*
28 *ys¹mẓʾwn w-s¹ẓyh*[… …]

to correct (see fig. 2):

26 *l-yrṯ ḫms¹y wrqm*
27 *l-mlk Qtbn w-ʿhr S²mr*
28 *ys¹mẓʾwn w-s¹ẓyy*

I translated (Avanzini 2004, 285): "must pay 50 pieces of gold to the king of Qatabān and the magistrate of *S²mr*. They will execute and regulate [… …]".
But surely the verbs at l. 28 are related to what precedes. There is no lacuna after the verbs. The inscription on the first face ended at l. 28 with *w-s¹ẓyy.*
We can translate: "let him pay a fine [different reading *l-yrṯ*, instead of *l-yḫrṯ*, but same meaning] of fifty (pieces of) gold to the king of Qatabān and the overseer of *S²mr*, who are (and will be) putting this into effect and let be known."

2. *yfʿl* without *b-* or *l-* after conjunctions
In QAT legal texts something similar to the construction already seen in the Early SAB legal texts seems to happen.
For instance:

(21) RES 3854, 8-9: *w-hmw ys¹s¹lb kbrn … f-l yʿtny mlkn* "but if the kabir is refusing … then let the king be responsible".

In the protasis we have: *yfʿl* = SAB *yfʿln.*

The verb in the prefixed form, without *b-* or *l-* is functional to the text syntax, connecting the action in the protasis with the jussive mode in the apodosis.
This is why I still prefer my translation of RES 4337A, 13-17 to the translations of A.F.L. Beeston and W.W. Müller.
For these two scholars in the lines 13-16 there is a clause of the edict and in the lines 16-21 another clause.
In my opinion, in the text there is a single clause: *w-mty yḫdr … w-mty l-yks³.*

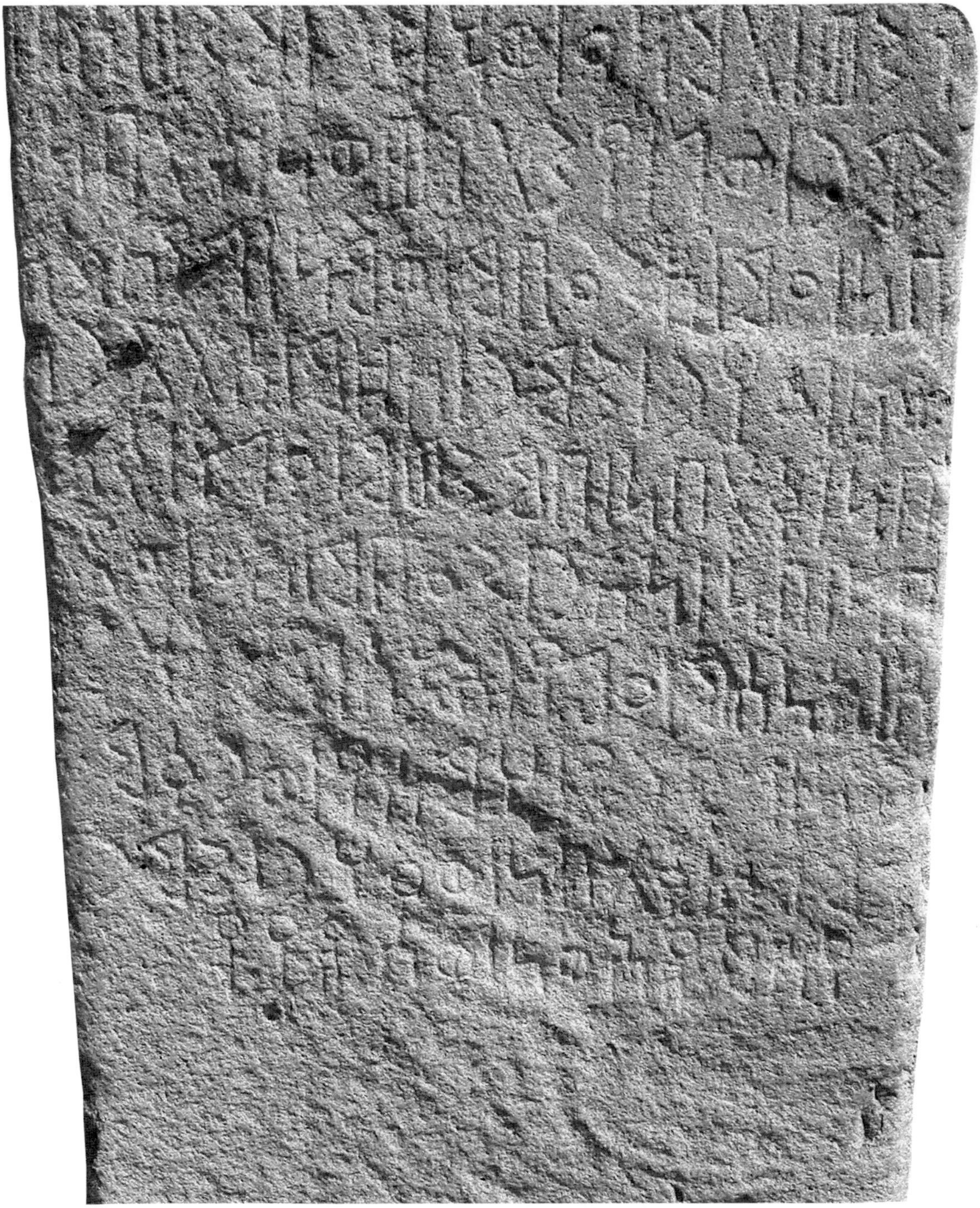

Figure 2 - RES 4337A (courtesy of Christian J. Robin).

(22) RES 4337A, 13-17:

13 *w-mty yḫdr ḫd-*
14 *rm w-ʾḏw b-ys*^{2}*tyṭ ʾw f-*
15 *tḫr b-ʿm kl ḏ-ḫdrm w-ms*^{2}*ṭ-*
16 *m blty ʿhr S*^{2}*mr w-mty*
17 *l-yks*^{3}*ʾ ʿhr S*^{2}*mr*

> And when such a one establishes a trading-stall thereafter he may either trade (on his own account) or enter into partnership with any (other) stallholder or merchant without the intervention of the overseer of *S*^{2}*mr*. And when the overseer of *S*^{2}*mr* announces that he desires … (Beeston 1959)
>
> *Und wenn er einen Laden besitzt, so treibe er dann Handel (für sich allein) oder tue sich zusammen mit jeglichem, der einen Laden hat und Händler ist, ohne den Aufseher von Schamir; und wenn der Aufseher von Schamir Kenntnis gib …* (Müller 1983)

In my opinion the text means: "And when he is opening a shop, a shopkeeper – that is a person who trades (by himself) or in association with any other shopkeeper or trades-person – without the permission of the magistrate of *S*^{2}*mr*, then the magistrate of *S*^{2}*mr* has to ratify …".

4. Sabaic *vs.* non-Sabaic languages

4.1. Innovative Sabaic *vs.* conservative non-Sabaic ?

The importance of the opposition *h/s* for a classification of ASA languages led P. Stein to underestimate the linguistic traits of SAB shared with the South Semitic.

For example, some common features with other ASA non-SAB languages are: the presence of declension, lost for North West Semitic languages from the first millennium and surely attested in QAT as well; the already mentioned *-k* ending for the first and second person of the imperfect, opposed to the *-t* ending of North West Semitic languages from the first millennium.

And again, SAB presents archaic traits, contrary to innovative linguistic traits of ASA non-SAB languages.

The tens, in SAB, are most probably formed with the ending of the dual (Stein 2003, 105), as in Akkadian – whereas ASA non-SAB languages present an ending in plural, as in Hebrew and in Aramaic (Avanzini *in press*); the ending for the third plural feminine person of the suffixed form of the verb is in *-y* (as in Akkadian), where other ASA non-SAB languages have *-n* as in Hebrew and Arabic (Avanzini 2006).

Yet again, the preposition *l* 'a' e *l-n* 'from' is an isogloss between SAB and Ugaritic.

For what concerns broken plurals a multiplicity of forms attested in SAB can be noticed that is certainly more varied than in non-SAB ASA languages. If we apply the rule defined by R. Hetzron (Hetzron 1976, 89): "the system that exhibits the most inner heterogeneity is likely to be the closest to the ancestor-system", it would be possible to formulate the hypothesis that the broken plural was initially a proto-SAB linguistic trait.

The diffusion of the broken plural might follow the opposite direction: from SAB to non-SAB languages, contrary to that proposed several times by P. Stein and N. Nebes going from non-SAB archaic languages to the innovative SAB.

I would never put forward as definite any hypothesis dealing with the possible acquisition process of the broken plural in southern Arabia. I simply wish to emphasize once again the risk that we take in transforming hypotheses in peremptory statements in the linguistic analyses of ASA languages.

4.2. Chronological and geographical distribution of the first attested written documents in Ancient South Arabian languages

The linguistic situation known at the beginning of history shows how the formation process of ASA languages was long and that, in the phase immediately preceding written documents, the language already showed important dialectal articulations.

In South West Arabia, in a relatively small region, there are attested languages with linguistic traits very different from one another.
As P. Stein legitimately claims, from minuscule texts and inscriptions there is evidence of languages co-existing, one next to the other, in some small areas, such as the Jawf.
At the beginning of the 8th century the ASA history began. The most important texts from Sirwah (DAI Ṣirwāḥ 2005-50, RES 3945, RES 3946) give an overview of the political articulation of southern Arabia in this period.
The cities of the Jawf, both independent or controlled by Saba', the cities in the region between the Jawf and the central area of Saba' reign (in the Wadi Raġwān), Marib, Qatabān and its capital, the regions in the Ḥaḍramawt, tribes and cities in the northern and southern plateau, Radmān, the tribe of Amir are mentioned.
All main actors in the future ASA history seem to be present in the 8th century.
But the direct documentation, in this century, is concentrated on few of these regions: in Marib, Ṣirwāḥ, and in the western area of Saba' (Wadi Raġwān, the Jawf). This area probably extended towards the Red Sea and Africa, if the SAB documentation of Tihama and Ethiopia dated back to the second half of the 8th century. Actually, some ^{14}C dating carried out by the German research group, suggest a date in the 9th/8th century for the Sabaean presence in Ethiopia.
The inscription of the *mukarrib* of Awsān (as-Saqqāf 1) is the only one that can be dated to the 8th century in the eastern part of Yemen. Until today, no documentation has been found from the Qatabanian and the Ḥaḍrami areas.
Qatabān certainly existed. Its capital was burned to the ground, Saba' imposed a king, but QAT documentation starts – somehow sporadically – at the beginning of the 7th century and remains quite limited up to the end of the 7th-beginning of the 6th century.
In the Jawf the texts are in MIN and in SAB since the first half of the 8th century; from the beginning of the documentation there are attested morphemes in *h* *vs.* morphemes in s^1.
This isogloss, as already said several times, is a diagnostic one, according to P. Stein, in order to propose a classification of ASA languages: SAB language on the one hand, non-SAB languages on the other.
Incidentally, it is wrong to indiscriminately insert the other three ASA languages in a generic non-SAB subgroup.
MIN, QAT and HAD present peculiar phonetic and morphologic traits. From a relatively long inscription, of unknown geographic provenance, it is possible to decide in which of the four ASA languages it was written and not only whether it was written in SAB or non-SAB.

4.3. 'Sabaeization' in the formative phase of the Ancient South Arabian culture

The classification SAB *vs.* non-SAB is functional for a case of contact attested in the documentation. Non-SAB languages undergo a process of 'Sabaeization', but there is no phenomenon occurring in the opposite direction in the formative phase of the ASA culture.
A centre of cultural dissemination between the end of the second millennium and the beginning of the first millennium, inside Yemen, must be hypothesized and its historical implications must be placed in the right perspective.
The documents attest the end of a process, but we do not know what happened in the previous phases. We must try to understand the historical conditions behind this process.

A.F.L. Beeston already considered as proof of the particular cultural prestige of Saba' the presence of the morpheme for the causative and of the suffixed pronoun with *-h* and not in *-s^1* in non-SAB inscriptions and in non-SAB onomastics.
The two phenomena (SAB morphemes in non-SAB languages and the 'Sabaic' onomastics) are to be kept separated even if they have, in my opinion, some implications between one another.
I would like to try and define the type of contact that led to the presence of morphemes in *h* in non-SAB languages in the formative phase of ASA culture.
The linguistic contact between uneven social groups (one more prestigious than the others) deals in the first instance with lexicon, in all known linguistic situations. The loan of a word is certainly easier than the loan of a morpheme.
This does not happen among ASA languages.
The study of non-SAB languages leads to the recognition of different lexicons compared to SAB. Excluding the common Semitic lexemes, present in all Semitic languages, the lexicon of the four ASA languages is strongly differentiated.
The linguistic 'Sabaeization' of other ASA languages deals only with morphology, or to be more precise, a single morphological trait: the suffixed pronouns and the prefixes of the causative.
A. Prioletta (Prioletta 2013, 96) and I. Rossi (Rossi 2014, 115) already noted that the presence of the *h* morpheme appears in different grammatical categories in the three non-SAB languages.
We are not simply dealing with a 'banal' contact among speakers of different languages, where the language of the socially weaker group is influenced by that of the more prestigious group.
In my opinion, the presence of the *h* morpheme in non-SAB languages, can be explained if placed in relation with the cultural and linguistic phenomenon of writing acquisition.
The beautifully geometric ASA writing cannot be born independently in the various areas of Yemen; it needs a disseminating centre.
Sometimes an important element is often underestimated: people learned writing only through oral teaching, nobody ever passed on a clay tablet, an ostracon, a wooden stick bearing a syllabary, an alphabet, to someone that had to learn how to write.
Writing was 'taught' to the populations of Yemen which Saba' has always been in contact with.
I think that the disseminating centre of writing, according to what is known today, must be in the Jawf, the key region for understanding the beginning of history and the linguistic situation in the first phase of the ASA states.
This is only a hypothesis, people are writing in Marib in the 8th century as well and it is certainly the central SAB writing school (in Marib, in Ṣirwāḥ), which, from the end of the century, will bring ASA writing towards a paradigmatic stylization on.
But the Jawf is the north-westernmost geographical area of ASA culture, the one, which was more open to contacts with the north.
P. Stein does not underestimate the importance of the Jawf in the most ancient phase of ASA history, even if the importance of the region is functional with his hypothesis of a general linguistic reconstruction.
In the Jawf, the newly arrived population speaking proto-SAB (or, as Stein 2012 a, 47 used to call them in a quite simplistic way: the Sabaeans) made contact with proto-MIN speaking people and adopted in their own language some linguistic traits typical of southern Semitic (*-k* and broken plurals).

This reconstruction, as already said several times, is ahistorical (there is no time for the long contact process) and unlikely on a sociolinguistic level.

The most interesting aspect of this region though is not limited to its contact with outside regions; the internal contact among some cities of the Jawf (speaking MIN) and the resourceful tribe of Saba' settled in other cities of the Jawf is of interest too.
Some years ago, Ch. Robin proposed to substitute MIN with 'Madhabaic'. The Minaean kingdom, based on the alliance between the cities of Maʿīn and Barāqish, was formed at the end of the 7th century. Ch. Robin felt it was incorrect to call MIN a language that was attested before the Minaean kingdom.
From a cultural point of view, as the Minaean kingdom gained strength, many things changed in the region (starting from the divine pantheon) but, on a linguistic level, no characteristic traits have been found that could justify a change in the name through which, over a long time, in general studies on Semitic languages, one of the four ASA languages has been identified.
I have suggested instead to use the 'Madhabaean/Madhabaic' label to indicate a period (8th and 7th century BC) and the documentation in MIN of some cities in the Jawf, before the formation of the Minaean kingdom.
During the 'Madhabaean' period the inhabitants of cities in the Jawf, who became rich through commercial exchanges, set the basis for a cultural identity, created an artistic style, and learned to write both in formal and in informal, private script.
The most ancient wooden sticks with minuscule script come from the Jawf, in particular from the city of Nashshān.
Incidentally, a typical trait of the ASA culture, which to be precise has no counterpart in the Old Aramaic or Canaanite epigraphy, is the creation, since the beginning, of two writing styles within the same alphabet: one used in public texts, the other for documents of everyday use. The Old Aramaic and Canaanite inscriptions are written in a minuscule script.
J. Pirenne was right in highlighting this phenomenon. Leaving aside comparisons with the Greek – loved by J. Pirenne – certainly, the creation of a formal, public script is one of the phenomena that characterize the culture of southern Arabia.
In this region, already from the first part of the 8th century, the ASA artistic style reached a notable expressive maturity. The canons of taste are fixed: the image is inserted inside a geometrical frame – either visually represented or imaginary – animals, plants, or geometric elements fill the space and frame the representations and texts.
I think that the region is key to the birth of the ASA culture and of its writing as well.
At the beginning of the first millennium the trade route that linked distant regions in Yemen existed already. Along this path not only merchants and goods went, but also scribes teaching how to write and promoting the creation of writing schools in the political structures of the eastern part of Yemen.
An intellectual contact, not only a commercial one, among ASA kingdoms certainly stands at the basis of the dissemination of writing in Yemen.
As years went by, non-SAB writing schools became autonomous from the Sabaean one, defining their own rules.
Also in the Jawf, when the time comes for the formation of the kingdom of Maʿīn, MIN documentation will show formularies and a palaeographic style that both differ from the Sabaean ones.

Teaching to write does not deal with a writing technique only, but also the syntactic and typological organization of the text, and of the specific stylistic features that have to be used. This holds true especially for the inscriptions.
ASA inscriptions present an organization of the text that can be easily analysed: a formulaic, stereotyped phraseology occurs at the beginning and at the end of the text. Inside the inscription, the text appears (relatively) freer.
In QAT and HAD the 'Sabaeisms' are present in the fixed frame of the text and in some textual typologies. The Sabaean scribe did not only teach how to write, but also which formularies had to be used in the frame of an epigraphic text.

4.4. 'Sabaeization' in the formative phase of the Ancient South Arabian culture in the Jawf

If the 'Sabaeization' is linked to the learning of writing, this should be less evident in the Jawf, where SAB and MIN have been close to one other since the beginning of history. Incidentally, from the beginning of the history of the kingdom of Maʿīn, we found several examples of 'Minaeism' in the SAB inscriptions from the Jawf. For example, in the SAB inscription B-L Nashq, in the beginning of the 6th century, we can find some lexical 'Minaeism': *rgl* "expedition", *mṣr w-rtkl* "he traded and led a caravan".
Indeed, MIN documentation is a sort of exception on its own.
In MIN neither the suffixed pronoun nor the causative verb in *h* are attested, excluding a case that I mention later on.
In MIN the *h* morpheme appears only in three nouns in *hfʿlt* form: *hḏmrt*, *hqnyt*, *hrwḥt*.
The nouns *hḏmrt* and *hrwḥt* are each attested in a single legal text (in M 168 and in al Jawf 04.28 respectively). The lexicon of a legal text is strongly characterized. In the Jawf, already in the 8th century, in the period of Sabaean-Madhabaean cultural *koiné*, legal texts were written. The two words may be a 'Sabaeism', even if *hḏmrt* has never been attested in SAB and *hrwḥt* is present only once in SAB – not by chance – in an Nashq inscription in the Jawf.
Nevertheless, *hḏmrt* and *hrwḥt* may also be two terms of the legal lexicon of the ancient Jawf. The form *hfʿlt* seems to identify an abstract noun: *hḏmrt* "to promulgate", *hrwḥt* "to enlarge", and not a concrete object.

The noun *hqnyt* actually seems to be a Sabaeism in MIN.
Even if that was the case, some notes could be added. In the 8th/7th centuries, in the central area of Saba', the dedication verb is *hqny*, but in the Jawf in the same period, in MIN inscriptions, the dedication verb is *s³l'*.
The inscription Kamna 30 (Arbach, Rossi 2015, 16-21) presents two dedicatory texts to the god Almaqah (one in SAB, the second one in MIN) written on the same slab. The SAB text has as author a Sabaean man, the MIN text has as author his wife from Kamna. In the SAB text the verb is: *hqny*, in the MIN text is: *s³l't*.
In Minaean inscriptions from the following centuries the verb *s³l'* does not disappear, and it is coordinated with *s¹qny* (never with *hqny*).
This observation has some interesting cultural implications.
The culture of the ancient Jawf is characterized by common traits. The formulae, in inscriptions both in MIN and in SAB from the Jawf, in the Madhabaean period, are often the same. For example *b-rʿẓ*: "upon will of", to introduce the name of the deity in final invocations in

dedicatory texts is attested only in the Jawf inscriptions of the ancient period, both in MIN and in SAB inscriptions. This is a choice related to cultural elements; one might say to a ‘fashion element’ inside the writing schools of a region, in a specific time period.
But the fact that the verb for ‘to dedicate’ was different in the two documentations, is a datum not banal at all. The verb is the principal verb for a typology of texts. It is strongly connoted, referring to the relationship between the worshiper and God. The Sabaeans and the Minaeans in the ancient Jawf preserve this difference.
Just in two SAB inscriptions from Haram we can find *s*^{3}*l’* and in my opinion not by chance.
From Haram comes a documentation that is linguistically complex and interesting. In the ancient period there are MIN and SAB inscriptions.
In the documentation of the beginning of the 7th century, *Yḏmrmlk*, king of Haram, is attested in two inscriptions, one in MIN and the other in SAB (Haram 12, and Haram 15).
The choice of a different language for two contemporary texts coming from the same city seems somehow related to the content of the texts. In the second inscriptions the alliance with Saba’ is celebrated and in the final invocations Almaqah is cited before the main god of Haram. The inscription is in SAB, but the Minaean cultural presence, strong in the city, is recognizable in the verb of dedication: *s*^{3}*l’*.
So, if we want find a proof that the Sabaeans are an ‘intrusive’ element in the Jawf, we can find it in the two different verbs for ‘to dedicate’. In the local, old tradition of the Jawf, the verb was *s*^{3}*l’*, *hqny* is arriving with the Sabaeans.
Indeed, in my opinion, the Sabaeans were arriving from Marib, not from Damascus!

Let us come back to *hqnyt*.
hqnyt is attested only in the inscriptions on the walls of Maʿīn and Barāqish in the final part of the text, in invocations to gods, after the verb *rṯd*: the author places his dedication under the protection of the gods.
In the documentation from Dedān, *hqnyt* is never attested, only *s*^{1}*qnyt*. This writing may be a hypercorrection, as argued by I. Rossi (Rossi, *in press*), or may be due to the fact that in Dedān there were no walls to be built and dedicated.
Beyond grammatical rules, textual typology influences linguistic choices.

As I said, in MIN there is only one attested example of a suffixed pronoun in *h* (*-hmy*) in an inscription (Moussaïeff 22, Bron 2008, 219-221) repeated on each of the pedestals of two bronze lions, commissioned by two kings of Nashshān.
The inscription presents, along with morphologic traits typical of MIN: *k-* preposition, pronoun suffixed with *s*^{1} (*’s*^{3}*l’-s*^{1}), also SAB elements: pronoun suffixed with *-hmy* (*s*^{2}*ʿb-hmy*). The dedication verb *s*^{1}*ḥdṯw* presents the prefix of the MIN causative *s*^{1} but marks, instead of the *scriptio defectiva*, typical of the MIN, the plural with *-w* ending.
This is a unique case in the epigraphic documentation of an inscription where different linguistic traits coexist ‘inside’ the same text. In the Jawf of the Madhabaean period, the inscriptions were written in MIN or in SAB.
With some imagination we can think that the artwork was made by a Sabaean artisan, and in the text there coexist at the same time some elements of the language of the author of the two bronze lions and of the language of the two dedicators.

4.5. 'Sabaeization' in the formative phase of the Ancient South Arabian culture in the Eastern part of Yemen

We do not know the mechanisms, the time that passed for the alphabetization of the Eastern kingdoms.
As I had already said from Awsān comes the only inscription (As-Saqqāf 1) in the 8th century. From a single inscription a great deal of imagination is needed to deduce general historical elements. Nevertheless, there are some data in the short text that are worth mentioning. Data which witness cultural contacts among different areas in Yemen.
The beginning of the text is:

(Ḏ)kr'(l) Lḥ[yn] (b)n ʿmkr(b) mkrb-'ws¹(n) [']*b Mrtʿm w-'byṯʿ*

First of all, the king of Awsān took the title of *mukarrib*. A cultural contact with Saba' is evident here.
The title of *mukarrib* is one of the traits that are common to the majority of the ASA culture and has no comparison in the rest of the Near East.
At first glance it seems credible to think that the institution behind the title of *mukarrib* was a Sabaean 'invention' that was passed on to the reign of Awsān.
The title of '*mukarrib* of *Dʿmt* and Saba'' can also be found in the SAB inscriptions from Ethiopia.
Even then, the lack of more information on the past of Awsān calls for a cautious approach.
The title is not attested in the Jawf, nor for Madhabiaean cities or for the Minaean reign.
The loan of this royal title might well have gone the other direction from Awsān to Saba'.

Then, in the onomastic formula of the *mukarrib* of Awsān there is an interesting trait: the *mukarrib* is "father of", an element in the onomastic formula that is attested only in the Madhabiaean period and, later on, in the Minaean period of the Jawf.
Apparently, it seems that there is not much difference between the expressions: "X father of" or "X and his sons." Actually, they address two different identity models.
I do not think it is a banal detail that in the inscription As-Saqqāf 1, the onomastic formula "X father of" is used; formula attested in the Jawf documentation and anywhere else in southern Arabia.
The onomastic formula suggests a contact between the Madhabiaean cities and the reign of Awsān, in the 8th century.

The contact with the Sabaean writing school is, for HAD documentation, relatively clear.
Even the decorations that accompany the text are influenced in Ḥaḍramawt, in the ancient period, by an artistic contact with Saba'.
In HAD the *h* morpheme is attested only in the documentation from the most ancient period: the *hqny* verb (also *hqnyt* and *hqnyw* are attested) and the suffixed pronoun *-hw* (neither *-hmw* nor *-hmy* or any other verb with the *h-* causative are attested).
Independent pronouns in HAD are formed on the root *s¹* (*s¹w*), the only productive one in the language. The presence of *hqny* and *-hw* is a calque from the SAB formulary in the writing learning phase.

Certainly, the QAT documentation presents the most numerous and articulated instances of the *h* morpheme.

In Qatabān the SAB writing school left evident and interesting traces.
To place the contact phenomenon between the Qatabanian and the Sabaean writing schools in the right perspective it would be useful to articulate the QAT documentation in a chronological way.
In the most ancient phase, the learning of writing and its formulae from Saba' is evident in QAT. Take, for example, the RES 3871 inscription.
Here, no *h* morpheme is mentioned but the presence of the SAB writing school model is graphically and linguistically there.
The text is a boustrophedon one, a *ductus* undoubtedly developed from the SAB writing school and much less attested outside Saba'. In RES 3871, before the citation of the Qatabanian pantheon, one can read: *qdm mbny Rydn mnḫy Ḥdnm* "he led the construction of *Rydn* towards *Ḥdnm*". The verb form in QAT should have been *tqdm*; moreover, *mnḫy* – which has to be interpreted as the preposition "towards" or a noun "canal" – is only attested in ancient SAB, without further examples in the subsequent SAB nor in QAT.
The presence of the Sabaean scribe in the writing of this text is evident.
In this period two verbs in the causative form in *h* are also attested: ...]*hqm-hw*, in the Ry 526 inscription, a fragmentary one, but written in boustrophedon ductus and certainly archaic, and *h'tw*, in Doe 1, most probably an archaic inscription though it is known only through a facsimile.

In the following period, the one I call B (B1 and B2), the verbs in the *h-* causative never appear in the QAT documentation, excluding a participial form which I am going to talk about further on (*mhnkrm*).
Various pronouns *-hw -hmw* are present in this period, in particular in inscriptions to celebrate the construction of buildings, written by the king or where he is cited in the final invocations. These are ideologically important inscriptions.
If we look at the suffixed pronouns attested I believe it clearly comes to light that the pronouns in *h* are not a productive element of QAT language.
As in HAD, the independent pronouns in QAT are in s^1.
From this point of view, the RES 4330 inscription is particularly interesting because all suffixed pronouns are in *h* (l. 2: *rṯd-hw*, l. 3: *wld-hw w-ḏ-ʿḏr-hw*, l. 4: *bn-hw*) except for the use of a proleptic genitive: "his land, the one of...", where $-s^1$ is used (l. 2: *l-'rḍ-*s^1 *ḏ-Drʿt*). There are not many examples in QAT of proleptic genitives, but for those that we have (e.g. "his month, the one of...") there is always the $-s^1$ pronoun.

If we pursue this analysis, more data emerge.
The suffixed pronoun *-hmw* is always suffixed to nouns, also *-hw* is normally suffixed to nouns excluding three examples, where *-hw* is suffixed to the verb *rṯd*.
The pronouns seem an integral part to the noun that comes before them, or of the verb *rṯd*. They are a fixed part of the text.
As I have already noted (Avanzini 1992, 16), suffixed pronouns or the causative prefix in *h* can always be found in QAT in lexemes that have a precise correspondence in the SAB lexicon.
The Qatabanian scribe learned which formulae to use, but whenever he enriches the formula with QAT lexical elements, he uses them in the correct form of his language.
In the curse formulae against whoever moves the inscription from the place where it was set,

two participles are used: *ms^{1}nkrm* and *ms^{1}fʾym*. The first verb is attested also in SAB, but the other is absent. There is in QAT the form *mhnkrm*, but never the **mhfʾym* one.
In Atlal 1, 11 and in FB-Ḥawkam 2, 10 we find: *mhnkrm w-ms^{1}fʾym*.

As usual, one should never be too rigid in formulating rules.
In the construction inscriptions, very often in this period, the pronoun in *-h* is suffixed to the nouns that indicate the various sections of the construction (e.g. Doe 6, 1-3: *byt-hw S^{2}bʿn w-ḫṭb-hw w-ms^{3}wd-hw w-ṣrḥty-hw w-gnʾy-hw w-fnwty-hw w-bʾr-hw glm*).
Among these examples we can find (though only once) *nfs^{1}hy-hw* (MQ-HK 4). This lexeme exists in SAB, but the grammatical form of the noun, external plural with *-hy* suffix, is QAT and not SAB.
In this case the scribe showed the ability to analyse the language, linking *-hw* with a word that was grammatically QAT.

In the period that followed in time (which I call period C) the pronouns in *h* disappear completely, also in the construction inscriptions that enumerate the sections of the construction and cite the king (e.g. Ja 119, 2-3: *byt-s^{1} Yfs^{2} w-kl ʾḫṭb-s^{1} w-ṣrḥt-s^{1}ww w-nfs^{1}h-s^{1}ww w-ms^{1}qft-s^{1} kl-s^{1}m glm*).
The prefix of the causative in *h-* is attested, in this period, very frequently in Marginal QAT (for a definition of Marginal Qatabanic, see Avanzini 2004, 513-514). In this case, for sure, we are dealing with a linguistic contact.
In central QAT we have a single inscription (MQ-Maqṣara al-Abraq 1), which presents two verbs in the causative form in *h-*: *hbrʾ* and *hnql*.
In this case, I think we are dealing with two very strange verbal forms.
hbrʾ is the causative form of *brʾ*, never attested anywhere else either in QAT or in SAB. *hnql* (in QAT is attested the noun *mnql* "pass", but not the verb *nql*) obviously refers to SAB.
In the inscription, the king *S^{2}hr Ygl Yhrgb*, one of the last great kings in Qatabān, is cited. *S^{2}hr Ygl Yhrgb* took the title of *mukarrib* and documentation citing his name is present on the plateau. We might think that the inscription MQ-Maqṣara al-Abraq must have been written by a scribe, who came from the plateau, a region, where the causative verbs in *h-* are present, as we already said before.
But verbs are too peculiar to accept such explanation without exceptions.
We might even assume that *hbrʾ* and *hnql* are two hyper-corrected forms.
In my opinion, a possible explanation for the scribe's choice can be found in a connotation of prestige given to the two verbal forms with *h* prefix, perceived by the scribe as an archaic form.

P. Stein accepts my hypothesis of the use, in QAT, of the *h* morpheme not related to uncertainty or superficiality from the scribe, but to fixed rules.
Once again, I wish to emphasize that these rules are writing norms and not grammatical ones.
I believe that it was not the QAT language that was affected by the political prestige of Sabaʾ, but it was the QAT writing school that remained close to the SAB school in some specific formularies and in particular text typologies.

With regard to the text typology, neither the *h* causative nor the *h* pronouns are ever attested in the QAT legal texts.

QAT legal texts are a very interesting typology and it is important to notice that no elements in *h* are ever attested here.

As I have already said (Avanzini *in press*), the RES 3858 inscription proves interesting, with the presence of the suffixed pronoun (l. 1: *hgr-hmw*, l. 2: *mlk-hmw*, etc., l. 14: *w-ʾrḍ-hw w-qny-hw l-hw w-l wld-hw w-ḏ-ʿḏr-hw*) and the causative in *h* (l. 1: *hṯb*) in the part of text that surrounds the actual legal text. In the legal part of the inscription (ll. 5-13), there are only pronouns in -s^1.

It is not surprising that in legal texts, as in modern legal texts, there are particular terms and a fixed phraseology. For example, the articulation of the norms cited is indicated in MIN and QAT by the enclitic -*ʾy*. This is attested in the two languages only in legal texts.

The most interesting aspect of legal texts, in my opinion, is that these texts seem freer in respect of the fixed formulae in which the writing schools inserted the text in the construction and dedicatory inscriptions

The legal text was initially written on perishable material (in the final formulae of texts it is mentioned that the text was written on stone and wood). We could think that this typology of text reflects the language spoken by the writer, more than the construction or dedicatory texts, which reflect the language of the writing school.

5. Onomastics

I have already stated beforehand that the morpheme *h* has nothing to do with a phenomenon of 'Sabaeization' (Avanzini 2006 a) when it is found inside a proper name, and even the latest studies by P. Stein did not change my mind.
It seems historically very unlikely that there were some 'local' onomastics in non-SAB Yemen regions, of which no proof has survived.

> *Auch wenn diese Sprachen* [non-SAB languages] *daneben ein eigenes, lokal geprägtes Onomastikon besassen, ist eine Orientierung am sabäischen Vorbild nicht zu übersehen.* (Stein 2012 a, 51)

There must have been fashions in choosing names for a child, but this has nothing to do with Stein's hypothesis. We do not have any proof of a 'local' onomastics in the non-Sabaean areas.
From my point of view, it is the peremptoriness of Stein's statements that should be criticized: in non-SAB proper names, where there are causative verbs or suffixed pronouns, these are in *h*, therefore such names are SAB.
It seems too easy to argue that as in ancient SAB onomastics a large percentage of theophoric names witnesses the presence of the Qatabanian god ʿAm, then it has to be deduced that ancient SAB onomastics is QAT.
Selecting an element, an isogloss, as basis for a whole linguistic and historical reconstruction is always dangerous and most of the times wrong.
ASA onomastics is conservative (typologically similar to the Amorite onomastics, and very different from the onomastics of North-West Semitic in the first millennium).
By resorting to the example cited above, if an inscription of which I do not know the provenance includes only the proper name of any ASA man or woman, not of a person with a special role such as the king, I can hypothesize – on the basis of metalinguistic elements only, like iconography and object typology – to which of the ASA linguistic regions it belongs.
But the proper name alone is not sufficient: it is an ASA name, not a SAB or non-SAB one.

In my opinion, onomastics is one of the 'common' elements within ASA culture, and dates back to the proto-historic phase.

6. Conclusions

Despite P. Stein's recent studies, which reformulate a hypothesis put forward by N. Nebes, I still find an endogenous formation model for ASA culture and languages more coherent with the linguistic and archaeological data known today. This endogenous process does not exclude, as hardly ever happens in ancient history, contacts with more culturally advanced regions.
There are no data in the archaeological and epigraphic sources able to support the hypothesis that the formation of ASA culture depended on the migration of populations.
The near contemporaneity of written alphabetical texts attested in the Syro-Palestinian area and in Yemen does not allow for the time span necessary to accept the arrival of foreign populations that settled and integrated with local populations.
Many of the linguistic and cultural elements common to the whole ASA cultural area formed thanks to an internal process that developed from an ancient proto-historic phase inside Yemen. Among these common elements, in my opinion, the ancient ASA onomastics of the Amorite type is worth noticing.
The articulation of ASA languages cannot be summed up in the opposition between innovative SAB and conservative non-SAB. SAB presents archaic traits that have not been preserved in non-SAB languages.
To place SAB in central Semitic *tout court*, because of the presence of the morpheme in *h* and of a supposed absence of the indicative/subjunctive opposition – thus leaving non-SAB languages in limbo of ignorance, as happened in recently published manuals of Semitic studies – seems wrong to me.
The classification of Semitic languages based on linguistic geography criteria, even before R. Hetzron as proposed by Ch. Rabin (Rabin 1963) and G. Garbini (Garbini 1972), is an important heuristic model that cannot become a dogma.
The selection of more significant isoglosses compared to less significant ones is often dangerous, especially when the number of isoglosses is very small.
In particular, I find the arguments of those who believe that the opposition *yənäggər/yəngär* does not have much to do with the Akkadian *iparras/iprus* very convincing.
But, even if we accept that the opposition in Ethiopic and in MSA must be connected to the Akkadian opposition thus becoming one of the diagnostic isoglosses to define Marginal Semitic, the absence of a yVqattVl form is not at all definitive in SAB.
A recent example cited by P. Stein himself: $ys^{2}ymn$ indicative *vs.* $ys^{2}mn$ subjunctive, might leave the discussion open once again.
It is not possible to be sure those graphical variations can be considered full/defective writing of morphologic variations. So, it is certainly wrong to consider as definitive some grammatical rules based on ambiguous data.

ASA languages present a complex linguistic situation, with archaic traits living side by side with innovative traits. Many of the isoglosses that characterize southern Semitic are present in SAB and MIN texts since the beginning of the first millennium BC.
Even if the arrival of the Sabaeans from afar is not at the basis of the formation of ASA culture, Sabaeans played a pivotal role in the most ancient period of ASA history.
ASA writing did not originate in the various ASA reigns independently, it developed from a centre and its dissemination needed an oral teaching.
Historically speaking, I wish to think that the dissemination centre of southern Arabian writing was the Sabaean and Madhabiaean Jawf, rather than the Marib area.
The political strength of Saba' reign in the second half of the 8th century, and the beginning of wars for territorial and commercial control could well have led to the development of the Sabaean writing school.
After the most ancient phase, HAD does not present the elements that refer to SAB writing school any more in epigraphic text writing.
In QAT the relationship between SAB writing school and the QAT school left long lasting interesting traces.
Even for QAT, I do not think that the presence of morphemes in *h*, a well-attested phenomenon that lasted for a long period and – for the sake of precision – in a commercially rich period of the reign, needs to be justified with the linguistic contact imposed by SAB, a more prestigious language, on QAT.
From texts it is possible to derive some rules for the use of the morpheme in *h* in QAT: these are writing rules, related to text typology.
The examples presented so far bear witness to the fact that Qatabanian and the Ḥaḍrami peoples learned to write from Sabaeans, but not that their languages – and even less their onomastics – mainly present a phenomenon of 'Sabaeization'.

References

Arbach M., Rossi I. 2015. Nouveaux documents sabéens provenant de Kamna du VIIIe–VIIe siècle avant J.-C., *Arabian Archaeology and Epigraphy* 26, 16-27.

Avanzini A. 1992. H-Forms in Qatabanian inscriptions, *Yemen. Studi archeologici, storici e filologici sull'Arabia meridionale* 1, 13-17.

Avanzini A. 2004. *Corpus of South Arabian Inscriptions I-III. Qatabanic, Marginal Qatabanic, Awsanite Inscriptions* (Arabia Antica, 2). Pisa: Edizioni Plus-Università di Pisa.

Avanzini A. 2006. To accompany a recently published Sabaic text: historical and grammatical remarks, pages 37-46 in P.G. Borbone, A. Mengozzi, M. Tosco (eds), *Loquentes linguis. Studi in onore di Fabrizio A. Pennacchietti*. Wiesbaden: Harrassowitz.

Avanzini A. 2006 a. Ancient South Arabian anthroponomastics: historical remarks, *Proceedings of the Seminar for Arabian Studies* 36, 79-85.

Avanzini A. 2009. Origin and classification of the Ancient South Arabian languages, *Journal of Semitic Studies* 54, 205-221.

Avanzini A. 2014. From inscriptions to grammar: notes on the grammar of non-Sabaic languages, pages 1-8. in O. Elmaz, J.C.E. Watson (eds), *Languages of Southern Arabia* (Supplement to the Proceedings of the Seminar for Arabian Studies, 44). Oxford: Archaeopress.

Avanzini A. *in press*. The inscription CSAI I, 203=RES 3858. Some observations on noun declension in the Qatabanic languages, in press in *Studies in honour of Ch. J. Robin*.

Beeston A.F.L. 1959. *The mercantile code of Qataban. Qahtan. Studies in Old Arabian Epigraphy*, 1. London: Luzac and Co.

Beeston, A.F.L. 1984. *Sabaic grammar* (Journal of Semitic Studies. Monograph, 6). Manchester: University of Manchester.

Bron F. 2008. L'inscription des lions de Nashshān, *Egitto e Vicino Oriente*, 31, 219-221.

Buffa V., Vogt B. 2001. Sabir – Cultural Identity between Saba and Africa, pages 437-450 in R. Eichmann, H. Parzinger (eds), *Migration und Kulturtransfer. Der Wandel vorder- und zentralasiatischer Kulturen im Umbruch vom 2. zum 1. vorchristlichen Jahrtausend. Akten des Internationalen Kolloquiums Berlin, 23. bis 26. November 1999* (Kolloquien zur Vor- und Frühgeschichte, 6). Bonn: Habelt.

Bunnens G. 2000. Syria in the Iron Age. Problems of Definition, pages 3-19 in G. Bunnens (ed.), *Essays on Syria in the Iron Age* (Ancient Near Eastern Studies, Supplement, 7). Louvain: Peeters Press.

Cohen D. 1984. *La phrase nominale et l'évolution du système verbal en sémitique. Études de syntaxe historique*. Leuven: Peeters.

Corriente F. 2013. Again on the classification of South-Semitic, pages 33-44 in J.P. Monferrer-Sala, W.G.E. Watson (eds), *Archaism and Innovation in the Semitic Languages* (Series Semitica Antiqua, 1). Cordoba: CNERU (Cordoba Near Eastern Research Unit) – DTR (Department of Theology and Religion, Durham University UK) – Oriens Academic.

Del Olmo Lete G. 2013. The Linguistic Continuum of Syria-Palestine in the Late II millennium BC, pages 113-127 in J.P. Monferrer-Sala, W.G.E. Watson (eds), *Archaism and Innovation in the Semitic Languages* (Series Semitica Antiqua, 1). Cordoba: CNERU (Cordoba Near Eastern Research Unit) – DTR (Department of Theology and Religion, Durham University UK) – Oriens Academic.

Drewes A.J., Higham T.F.G., Macdonald M.C.A., Ramsey C.B. 2013. Some absolute dates for the development of the Ancient South Arabian Script, *Arabian Archaeology and Epigraphy* 24, 196-207.

Fales F.M. 2011. Old Aramaic, pages 555-573 in S. Weninger *et alii* (eds), *The Semitic Languages. An International Handbook* (Handbücher zur Sprach- und Kommunikations-wissenschaft, 36). Berlin-Boston: De Gruyter Mouton.

Garbini G. 1972. *Le lingue semitiche. Studi di storia linguistica.* Napoli: Istituto Orientale.

Garr W.R. 1985. *Dialect Geography of Syria-Palestine 1000-586 B.C.E.* Philadelphia: University of Pennsylvania Press.

Gruntfest Y. 1999. The consecutive imperfect in Semitic epigraphy, pages 171-189 in Y. Avishur, R. Deutsch (eds), *Michael: historical, epigraphical and biblical studies in honor of Prof. Michael Heltzer*. Tel Aviv: Archaeological Center Publications.

Hasselbach R. 2012. Old South Arabian, pages 160-193 in H. Gzella (ed.), *Languages from the World of the Bible*. Berlin: de Gruyter.

Hetzron R. 1974. La division des langues sémitiques, pages 181-194 in A. Caquot, D. Cohen (eds), *Actes du premier congrès international de linguistique sémitique et camito-sémitique, Paris 16-19 Juillet 1969*. The Hague, Paris: Mouton.

Hetzron R. 1976. Two principles of Genetic Reconstruction, *Lingua* 38, 89-104.

Huehnergard J. 2005. Features of Central Semitic, pages 155-203 in A. Gianto (ed.), *Biblical and Oriental Essays in Memory of William L. Moran* (Biblica et Orientalia, 48). Rome: Pontificio Istituto Biblico.

Huehnergard J., Rubin A.D. 2011. Phyla and Waves: Models of Classification of the Semitic Languages, pages 259-278 in S. Weninger *et alii* (eds), *The Semitic Languages. An International Handbook* (Handbücher zur Sprach- und Kommunikations-wissenschaft, 36). Berlin-Boston: De Gruyter Mouton.

Kottsieper I., Stein P. 2014. Sabaic and Aramaic – a common origin?, pages 81-88 in O. Elmaz, J.C.E. Watson (eds), *Languages of Southern Arabia. Papers from the Special Session of the Seminar for Arabian Studies held on 27 July 2013* (Supplement to the Proceedings of the Seminar for Arabian Studies, 44). Oxford: Archaeopress.

Macdonald M.C.A. 2015. On the uses of writing in ancient Arabia and the role of palaeography in studying them, *Arabian Epigraphic Notes* 1, 1-50.

de Maigret A. 1990. *The Bronze Age Culture of Khawlān aṭ-Ṭiyāl and Al-Ḥadā (Yemen Arab Republic). A First General report* (Reports and Memoirs, 24). Rome: IsMEO.

Mazzini G. 2005. Ancient South Arabian documentation and the reconstruction of Semitic', pages 215-238 in P. Fronzaroli, P. Marrassini (eds), *10th meeting of Hamito-Semitic Linguistics, Firenze 18-21 Aprile 2001* (Quaderni di Semitistica, 25). Florence: Università di Firenze.

Mouton M., Schiettecatte J. 2014. *In the Desert Margins. The Settlement Process in the ancient South and East Arabia* (Arabia Antica, 9). Rome: «L'Erma» di Bretschneider.

Müller W.W. 1983. Altsüdarabische Dokumente, pages 268-282 in D. Conrad (ed.). *Dokumente zum Rechts- und Wirtschaftsleben.* O. Kaiser (ed.), *Texte aus der Umwelt des Alten Testaments.* 1.3. Gütersloh: Gütersloher Verlagshaus Gerd Mohn.

Nebes N. 1994. Zur Form der Imperfekt-basis des unvermehrten Grundstammes in Altsüdarabishen, pages 59-81 in W. Heinrichs, G. Schoeler (eds), *Festschrift Ewald Wagner zum 65. Geburtstag.* Bd. 1. *Semitische Studien unter besonderer Berücksichtigung der Südsemitistik* (Beiruter texte und Studien, 54). Beirut: in Kommission bei Franz Steiner Verlag Stuttgart.

Nebes N. 1994 a. *Verwendung und Funktion der Präfixkonjugation im Sabäischen*, pages 191-211 in N. Nebes (ed.), *Arabia Felix. Beiträge zur Sprache und Kultur des vorislamischen Arabien. Festschrift Walter W. Müller zum 60. Geburtstag.* Wiesbaden: Harrassowitz Verlag.

Nebes N. 2001. Zur Genese der altsüdarabischen Kultur. Eine Arbeitshypothese, pages 427-435 in R. Eichmann, H. Parzinger (eds), *Migration und Kulturtransfer. Der Wandel vorder- und zentralasiatischer Kulturen im Umbruch vom 2. zum 1. vorchristlichen Jahrtausend. Akten des internationalen Kolloquiums Berlin, 23. bis 26 November 1999* (Kolloquien zur Vor- und Frühgeschichte, 6). Bonn: Habelt.

Nebes N. 2007. Ita'amar der Sabäer. Zur Datierung der Monumentalinschrift des Yiṯaʿʾamar Watar aus Ṣirwāḥ, *Arabian Archaeology and Epigraphy* 18, 25-33.

Nebes N. 2011. Der Tatenbericht eines sabäischen Mukarribs als Widmungsinschrift, pages 362-367 in *Texte aus der Umwelt des Alten Testaments.* Neue Folge, 6. Gütersloh: Gütersloher Verlagshaus.

Prioletta A. 2006. Note di epigrafia Hadramawtica 1. L'alternanza di *ṯ* e *s*^{3}, *Egitto e Vicino Oriente* 29, 249-267.

Prioletta A. 2013. Remarks on some processes of assimilation and innovation in the language and culture of Ḥaḍramawt during its ancient history, *Aula Orientalis* 31, 93-108.

Rabin Ch. 1963. The Origin of the Subdivisions of Semitic, pages 104-115 in D. Winton Thomas, W.D. McHardy (eds), *Hebrew and Semitic Studies presented to G.R. Driver.* Oxford: Oxford University Press.

Robin Ch. J. 2008. La lecture et l'interprétation de l'abécédaire de Ra's Shamra 88.2215. La preuve par l'Arabie ?, pages 233-244 in C. Roche (ed.), *D'Ougarit à Jérusalem. Recueil d'études épigraphiques et archéologique offert à Pierre Bordreuil.* Parigi: de Boccard.

Rossi I. 2014. The Minaeans beyond Maʿīn, pages 111-124 in O. Elmaz, J.C.E. Watson (eds), *Languages of Southern Arabia* (Supplement to the Proceedings of the Seminar for Arabian Studies, 44). Oxford: Archaeopress.

Rossi I. *in press*. Between north and south: the Minaic documentation from al-ʿUlā, in press in *Le contexte de naissance de l'écriture arabe: Écrit et écritures araméennes et arabes au 1er millénaire après J.-C., Proceedings of the colloquium held in Paris, 4th-6th April 2013, CNRS-UMR Orient et Méditerranée.*

Schiettecatte J. 2011. *D'Aden à Zafar. Villes d'Arabie du Sud préislamique* (Orient et Méditerranée, 6). Paris: de Boccard.

Stein P. 2003. *Untersuchungen zur Phonologie und Morphologie des Sabäischen* (Epigraphische Forschungen auf der Arabischen Halbinsel, 3). Rahden/Westf.: Marie Leidorf GmbH.

Stein P. 2010. *Die altsüdarabischen Minuskelinschritfen auf Holzstäbchen aus der Bayerishen Staatsbibliotek in München* (Epigraphische Forschungen auf der Arabischen Halbinsel, 5). Tübingen: Wasmuth.

Stein P. 2011. Ancient South Arabian, pages 1042-1073 in S. Weninger *et alii* (eds), *The Semitic Languages. An International Handbook* (Handbücher zur Sprach- und Kommunikationswissenschaft, 36). Berlin-Boston: de Gruyter Mouton.

Stein P. 2012. Sabaica – Aramaica (1), pages 503-522 in T. Polański (ed.), *Studia Andreae Zaborski Dedicata* (Folia Orientalia, 49). Cracow: Polish Academy of Sciences.

Stein P. 2012 a. Aspekte von Sprachbewusstsein im antiken Südarabien, pages 29-58 in J. Thon, G. Veltri, E.-J. Waschke (eds), *Sprachbewusstsein und Sprachkonzepte im Alten Orient, Alten Testament und rabbinischen Judentum* (Orientwissenschaftliche, 30). Halle: Zentrum für Interdisziplinäre Regionalstudien (ZIRS).

Tropper J. 1997. Subvarianten und Funktionen der sabäischen Präfixkonjugation, *Orientalia* 66, 34-57.

Vogt B., Sedov A. 1998. The Sabir culture and coastal Yemen during the second millennium BC. The present state of discussion, *Proceedings of the Seminar for Arabian Studies* 28, 261-270.

Vogt B., Sedov A., Buffa V. 2002. Zur Datierung der Sabir-Kultur, pages 27-39 in *Archäologische Berichte aus dem Yemen* 9. Mainz am Rhein: Verlag Philipp von Zabern.

Voigt R. M. 1987. The classification of Central Semitic, *Journal of Semitic Studies* 32, 1-21.

Wilkinson T. J. 2005. The Other Side of Sheba: Early Towns in the Highlands of Yemen, *Bibliotheca Orientalis* 62, 5-14.

Wilkinson T. J., Edens C., Gibson M. 1997. The Archaeology of the Yemen High Plains: a Preliminary Chronology, *Arabian Archaeology and Epigraphy* 8, 99-142.